STEVE BACKSHALL'S
2017 Annual
A YEAR OF ADVENTURE

Steve checking out a polar bear kill in the Arctic.

STEVE BACKSHALL'S
2017 Annual
A YEAR OF ADVENTURE

ORION CHILDREN'S BOOKS

First published in Great Britain in 2016
by Hodder and Stoughton

13 5 7 9 10 8 6 4 2

Photo credits (b: bottom; t: top; l: left; r: right; c: centre)

Steve Backshall: 4-5; 6-7; 10; 17; 25; 33; 41; 51; 54tl. **Ardea:** 30tr Andrey Zvoznikov; 30cl M. Watson; 31bl Dante Fenolio/Science Sour; 49tl Frans Lanting/Danita Delimont. **Dollarphotoclub:** 31tl Francesco de Marco. **Shutterstock:** 2-3 Brandelet; 9 Bppix; 12-13 2630ben; 14tl Andrzej Kubik; 14br, SantiPhotoSS; 15tl Krzysztof Odziomek; 15cr Svoboda Pavel; 15cl Karel Gallas; 15br Cherryson; 16tl Boris Pamikov; 16cr Karel Gallas; 16bl Erni; 18bl Martin Mecnarowski; 18c Gudkov Andrey; 19 GG StudiosAustria; 20-21 Leonardo Gonzalez; 22tr Holbox; 22bl BMJ; 22br Vilainecrevette; 23tl Cosmin Manci; 23tr Ryan M. Bolton; 23bl Tom Reichner; 24tl Jordi Roy; 24cr Andrea Izzotti; 24bl Red Squirrel; 24br Gianluca Rasile; 26l JHVEPhoto; 26r WayneDuguay; 27 Targn Pleiades; 28-29 Vladimir Wrangel; 30br Florian Andronache; 31cr Joost van Uffelen;32tl Greg Amptman; 32cr Eric Isselee; 32bl Martin P; 34bl and 34c Mark Higgins; 36-37 Holly Kuchera; 38bl Dangdumrong; 38tr Erni; 38br Joe McDonald; 39cl Hilton; 39tr Pim Leijen; 39br Eduard Kyslynskyy; 40tl Peter Waters; 40tl inset Calvin Ang; 40cr Rujithai; 40bl Ryan M. Bolton; 42l Greg Amptman; 42r Photon75; 43 Michael Rothschild; 44-45 D and D Photo Sudbury; 46 Gudkov Andrey; 47tc Rich Carey; 47tl Norm Diver; 47tl inset Heiko Kiera; 47br Plavevski; 48tl Nagel Photography; 48tr Lee Prince; 48bl Jonathan Pledger; 49tr Robbie Taylor; 49b ArCaLu; 50tl Talvi; 50bl Brandelet; 50cr Nicolasvoisin44; 52 Nomad-photo.eu; 53 Sergey Uryadnikov; 54cl Kotomiti Okuma; 54bl 44kmos; 54cr Patrick Rolands; 55tl Claudia Otte; 55c Master1305; 55b Michael Rothschild; 56tr Seb c'est bien; 56b Martin P; 57 Dennis W. Donohue; 60tl Dmytro Zinkevych; 60br Artphotoclub; 60-61 Hugh Lansdown; 62-63 Brandelet.

Compiled by Jinny Johnson
Designed by Sue Michniewicz

A CIP catalogue record for this book
is available from the British Library.

ISBN 978 1 5101 0156 2

MIX
Paper from
responsible sources
FSC® C104740

Printed and bound in China

The paper and board used in this
book are from well-managed
forests and other
responsible sources.

Orion Children's Books
An imprint of Hachette Children's Group
Part of Hodder and Stoughton
Carmelite House 50 Victoria Embankment London EC4Y 0DZ

An Hachette UK Company
www.hachette.co.uk

www.hachettechildrens.co.uk

CONTENTS

WELCOME TO STEVE BACKSHALL'S 2017 ANNUAL

A YEAR OF ADVENTURE

I've been lucky enough to travel all over the world, filming my programmes and finding about wildlife, but there is always more to discover. Animals never fail to amaze and surprise me.

In this annual I've loads more to tell you about animals – how big they are, how they move around and find food, and how they look after their young. There's also a chapter about something that really concerns me – the many wonderful creatures that are becoming increasingly rare, why this is happening and how you can help them and make a difference.

As always there are also lots of pictures and some fun puzzles for you to enjoy, so please join me on another wonderful trip through the natural world.

The bird with the longest wings is the **wandering albatross**. Its wings measure an amazing 3.5 metres from tip to tip.

The **kori bustard** is one of the heaviest of all flying birds. It weighs up to 19 kilos.

The longest of all snakes is the **reticulated python**, which can measure up to 9 metres – more than a line of 5 tall people lying head to toe.

The biggest frog is the **goliath frog**, which lives in West Africa. It can grow to more than 30 centimetres long and weigh over 3 kilos.

The heaviest animal that has ever lived is the **blue whale**. It can weigh up to 120 tonnes.

CHAPTER 1

BIGGEST, LONGEST, HEAVIEST

The **African elephant** has the biggest brain of any land animal – it weighs up to 5.4 kilos. A human brain weighs about 1.3 kilos.

THE FACTS

An elephant's tusks are actually teeth so are probably the longest teeth of any animal. But these tusks are outside the elephant's mouth. **Hippos** also have very big teeth – and they are inside the mouth. The two huge teeth in the lower jaw can be as much as 30 centimetres long, and that is just the part you can see above the gum. A hippo's tooth can weigh three kilograms, as much as three big bags of sugar.

Hippos feed mostly on plants, but males do use their enormous teeth as weapons to threaten or fight off rivals.

The **giraffe** is the tallest animal in the world. An average male giraffe is about 5.3 metres tall – it could look over the top of a London double-decker bus! Even a newborn baby giraffe measures about 1.8 metres – as much as a tall human.

A giraffe's neck is 2.4 metres long but it doesn't have any extra bones. It has seven neck bones, just like we do, but each bone is 25 centimetres long.

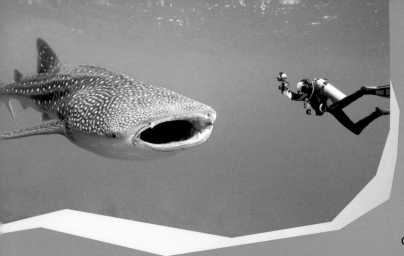

Imagine having a tongue that's as long as your whole body! That's what a **chameleon** has. A chameleon is a kind of lizard. When it's not hunting prey, the chameleon keeps its tongue hidden away in its mouth. But when it spots something good to eat it shoots out its tongue to catch its meal. The prey is trapped on the sticky tip of the tongue and then swiftly pulled back into the chameleon's mouth.

The biggest shark in the world is the **whale shark**, not the great white. The whale shark is also the world's biggest fish and is 12 metres long, about the same as a line of three average cars. Despite its huge size, the whale shark is not a fierce hunter. This giant feeds on huge numbers of tiny sea creatures called plankton that float in the ocean.

Stag beetles are probably the biggest insects living in Britain – and certainly some of the most exciting. The male has huge jaws shaped like antlers that it uses to fight or show off to other males. The male can be up to 7.5 centimetres long – as much as a grown-up person's finger.

The **emperor penguin** is the biggest of all penguins. It stands about 1.2 metres high – as tall as an average seven-year-old child. The emperor lives in Antarctica and hunts prey such as fish and squid.

One of the world's largest jellyfish is the **lion's mane jellyfish**. Its bell-shaped body measures as much as two metres across – a tall adult human could stretch out on it! It has as many as 150 tentacles hanging from its body and these can be 60 metres long. This giant catches small fish and other sea creatures – as well as smaller jellyfish – with its stinging tentacles.

All of the five kinds of rhino are big animals but the largest is the **white rhinoceros**, which lives in southern and central Africa. A male is up to 4 metres long with a 70-centimetre tail, and weighs 2.3 tonnes. Rhinos feed on huge amounts of grass.

The **badger** is Britain's largest land carnivore (meat-eating mammal). A male is about 75 centimetres long with a tail of about 15 centimetres and weighs up to 12 kilos. Although badgers are carnivores, they will eat almost anything, including nuts, fruit, and earthworms. Badgers have short strong legs and long claws that help them dig burrows for shelter.

The animal with the longest claws is not a bear, not a tiger but the **giant armadillo**. This mammal has huge claws and the third claw on each front foot can measure more than 20 centimetres. The armadillo uses its strong claws to dig into termite mounds so it can eat up the insects inside.

Male **southern elephant seals** are the largest seals. These seals live in the seas around Antarctica and they are huge! A male weigh as much as 3,700 kilograms – more than 46 people. The female is much smaller – up to about 900 kilos. The male also has an extra-large snout called a proboscis that it can puff up to make its roars louder.

STEVE BACKSHALL'S BIGGEST, LONGEST, HEAVIEST WORDSEARCH

The names of 12 of the animals mentioned in this chapter are hidden in this wordsearch puzzle. Can you find them all?

s	e	s	a	a	o	r	e	b	b	s	w	h	g	a
h	o	o	n	p	d	f	o	l	i	e	h	i	t	e
g	u	r	t	t	f	l	u	a	i	d	a	p	m	e
o	p	a	e	a	l	e	r	t	n	n	l	p	u	y
r	i	d	r	c	w	u	s	s	t	o	e	o	l	r
i	e	i	t	h	o	l	n	a	e	r	s	p	t	e
l	g	r	a	e	r	n	r	i	o	g	h	o	n	g
l	i	l	a	o	o	m	i	r	b	e	a	t	a	d
a	e	s	n	n	a	t	p	h	t	u	r	a	h	a
h	l	u	r	d	i	e	t	e	r	t	k	m	p	b
o	r	t	i	m	n	c	p	y	i	e	t	u	e	e
h	a	l	h	g	e	t	e	h	r	h	t	s	l	p
h	l	i	u	a	l	w	d	s	o	h	e	i	e	m
o	i	i	s	s	o	r	t	a	b	l	a	o	h	a
o	n	s	t	a	g	b	e	e	t	l	e	e	s	w

Blue whale, Elephant, Giraffe, Hippopotamus, Whale shark, White rhinoceros, Giant armadillo, Gorilla, Badger, Emperor penguin, Stag beetle, Albatross

STEVE'S SPOTLIGHT ON . . .
EASTERN GORILLA

Monkeys, apes and humans all belong to a group of mammals called primates, and the largest of all the primates is the eastern gorilla. At up to 1.7 metres tall and weighing 160 kilos, this great ape is slightly bigger then its close relative, the western gorilla.

There are two kinds of eastern gorilla – mountain gorillas and eastern lowland gorillas – and both live in parts of East Africa. Both are rare and there are probably only about 880 mountain gorillas left in the wild.

You might think that these powerful animals are ferocious hunters but

they are not. Gorillas are plant-eaters and they feed mostly on leaves, stems, berries and fruit – though they may gobble up a few insects as well. They spend much of the day eating and at night sleep in nests made of branches and leaves. Each gorilla makes a fresh nest every night, but a baby shares its mother's nest.

Gorillas live in family groups, led by a large male – male gorillas are much bigger than females. Gorillas are usually peaceful animals, but a male will fiercely defend his family if threatened and he will shout, scream and even charge at enemies.

A family troop includes several females and their young. A newborn baby gorilla weighs about 2 kilos and is able to walk at about eight months old. Young gorillas are very well cared for by their mums and stay close for about four years, but when they are fully grown and mature they must leave. Young males set up their own family. Females find a troop to join.

A gorilla's arms are longer than its legs.

Humans have unique fingerprints but each gorilla has its own nose print! The pattern of wrinkles on the nose is different on every gorilla.

A gorilla usually walks on all fours but can walk upright for a few metres.

The lifespan of a gorilla is 30–40 years.

A **red kangaroo** can bound along at up to 64 kilometres an hour.

A **polar bear** can run at 40 kilometres an hour for short distances. It swims at about 6.5 kilometres an hour.

The **eider duck** can reach speeds of 76.5 kilometres an hour and keep going for long periods of level flight.

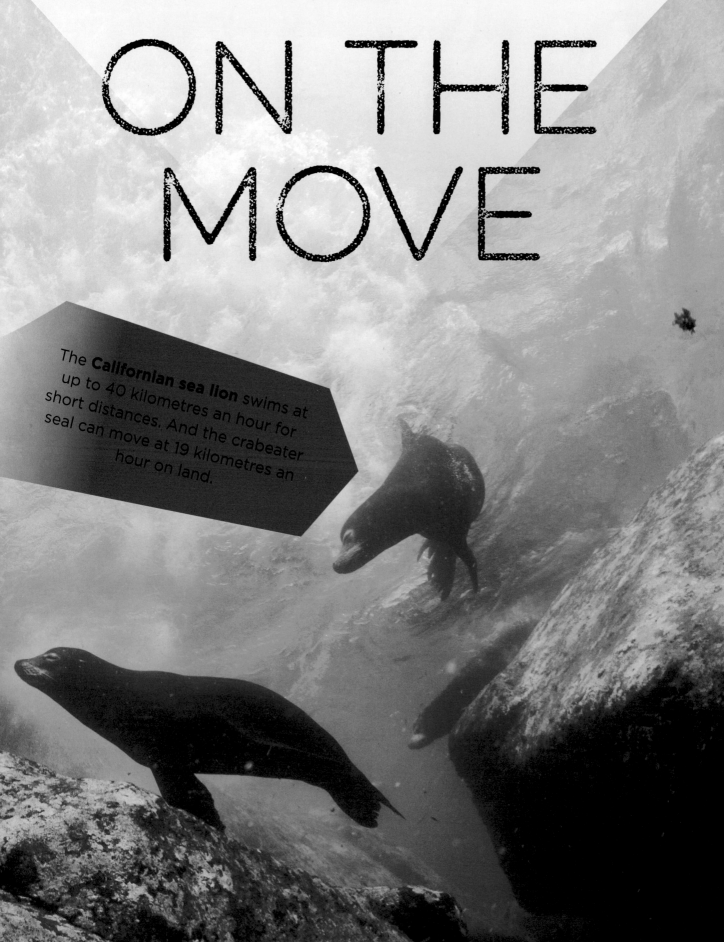

CHAPTER 2

ON THE MOVE

The **Californian sea lion** swims at up to 40 kilometres an hour for short distances. And the crabeater seal can move at 19 kilometres an hour on land.

THE FACTS

Tiny hummingbirds beat their wings faster than any other bird. As the wings beat, they make the humming sound that has given the birds their name. The **horned sungem hummingbird** beats its wings an incredible 90 times a second as it hovers in front of flowers, feeding on sweet nectar.

Hovering uses up lots of energy so hummingbirds need to visit 2,000 or more flowers a day to get enough food. Each day they eat as much as one and a half times their body weight of nectar.

The **Arctic tern** flies from the Arctic, where it breeds in summer, to Antarctica where it spends the other half of the year. It may travel as far as 40,000 kilometres every year.

The **bluefin tuna** is one of the fastest of all fish and swims at 70 kilometres an hour or more for short distances. Other fast swimmers are the marlin, the wahoo and the sailfish.

Sloths are some of the slowest-moving of all animals. They live in Central and South American rainforests and spend 15 hours or more a day sleeping. When a sloth does move, it's very, very slow – travelling about 36 metres a day. That's less than the width of a football pitch.

Sloths spend most of their time high in the trees, feeding on leaves. About once a week they make their way down to the ground to do a poo!

A **cat flea** is smaller than a grain of rice – but it can leap an astonishing 34 centimetres into the air. A flea has to be able to leap up on to a cat so it can live in its fur and feed on its blood.

The cheetah is the fastest land animal for short sprints, but the **pronghorn**, or American antelope, does better over long distances. The pronghorn's top speed is about 86 kilometres an hour and it can keep going at 56 kilometers an hour for six kilometers.

Flying frogs don't really fly but they can glide as far as 15 metres from branch to branch. These frogs live in Southeast Asian rainforests where the trees are very tall. Gliding from tree to tree is much quicker and easier than going all the way down to the ground!

When a frog leaps, it spreads out its webbed feet and the flaps of skin on its heels and elbows. These act like a parachute to slow the frog's fall. The frog steers itself by moving its legs.

Bats are the only mammals that can truly fly. One of the speediest of all bats is the **Mexican free-tailed bat**. It flies at 75 kilometres an hour but can reach speeds of more than 96 kilometres an hour with good tail winds. Its unusually long, narrow wings may help it fly at speed. This bat tends to fly farther, higher and for longer than other kinds of bat as it searches for insects to eat.

Little **Alpine swifts** travel thousands of kilometres every year as they migrate between Europe and Africa. Scientists have discovered that they spend an incredible 200 days at a stretch in the air, never coming to land. The swifts catch and eat insects while on the wing and may even sleep in the air for brief periods.

The **death's head hawk-moth** is one the fastest flying of all butterflies and moths. It's said to move at more than 50 kilometres an hour for short distances and regularly flies at 24 kilometres an hour.

This moth also makes a very strange squeaking sound, using special mouthparts that work in a similar way to an accordion.

Many whales are deep divers and one of the champions is the **Cuvier's beaked whale.** This whale has been tracked diving to 2,992 metres – that's nearly 3 kilometers. The dive lasted over 137 minutes.

The **house centipede** has 15 pairs of legs so you would expect it to be a fast mover. It is only a few centimetres long, but can bustle along at about 1.8 kilometres an hour.

The **brown hare** depends on speed to escape from predators such as foxes, buzzards and owls and can run at up to 70 kilometres an hour. Its long back legs help it move fast.

STEVE BACKSHALL'S
ON THE MOVE
WORDSEARCH

The names of 12 of the animals mentioned in this chapter are hidden in this wordsearch puzzle. Can you find them all?

o	j	w	c	w	z	s	w	a	g	s	b	n	j	d
s	d	r	g	g	o	k	s	o	u	l	r	i	g	n
w	i	u	s	a	f	n	r	r	z	o	o	b	h	r
t	z	t	t	j	n	f	j	x	u	t	w	a	f	e
c	e	e	e	f	g	n	g	x	o	h	n	a	n	t
a	n	u	t	n	i	f	e	u	l	b	h	e	u	c
w	i	l	i	k	x	w	h	t	t	u	a	l	b	i
f	f	y	u	e	s	n	s	t	o	v	r	f	c	t
n	l	i	o	v	p	h	g	e	o	m	e	t	z	c
f	p	r	o	n	g	h	o	r	n	m	l	a	d	r
r	a	e	b	r	a	l	o	p	f	i	k	c	w	a
c	h	e	e	t	a	h	v	i	u	v	p	w	a	l
m	x	v	l	m	e	f	t	n	m	l	t	l	a	o
p	s	i	z	e	r	t	y	r	m	z	v	q	a	h
x	v	e	i	y	s	s	h	k	o	t	n	v	z	q

Bluefin tuna, Arctic tern, Sloth, Cat flea, Cheetah, Pronghorn, Flying frog
Hawk-moth, Alpine swift, Brown hare, Gannet, Polar bear'

STEVE'S SPOTLIGHT ON . . .
NORTHERN GANNET

The gannet is a large seabird seen on coasts and islands on both sides of the North Atlantic. It spends much of its time flying over the sea, but colonies of thousands of birds gather on cliffs and islands to nest and lay their eggs.

The gannet feeds on fish, which it catches by making spectacular dives into the sea. As it flies high above the water, the gannet watches for schools of fish such as herring and mackerel. Once it sights something, the bird folds back its wings and holds its long beak straight out in front. In this position it dive-bombs its prey, plunging almost vertically into the water at speeds of up to 100 kilometres an hour. The gannet briefly disappears under the surface, seizes its prey, then pops back up. It may eat its catch underwater or bring it to the surface.

The impact of this high-speed entry into the water is cushioned by air sacs – similar to bubble wrap – at the front of the bird's body. These inflate to help to absorb the shock. Also the gannet does not have external nostrils – if it did water would be forced into them as it dives into the sea at great speed. Instead this bird has slits at the sides of the beak that close off when it dives.

Sometimes huge flocks of as many as 1,000 gannets gather to dive-bomb prey together.

Dives up to 22 metres below the surface when chasing prey.

Plumage mostly white with black tips to the wings.

Body is about 90 centimetres long.

Long narrow wings measure up to 1.9 metres from tip to tip.

A newborn **giant panda** weighs only 85-140g – about the same as an apple. Its mother is about a thousand times heavier than her tiny baby.

The **bee humming bird** is one of the smallest of all birds and it lays tiny eggs. They are only 6 millimetres long – about the same as an apple pip.

An **African elephant**'s pregnancy lasts for about 22 months. A newborn elephant weighs 90-120 kilos and is able to stand only 30 minutes after its birth.

CHAPTER 3

ANIMAL FAMILIES

The **ostrich** is the world's biggest bird and it lays the largest eggs. An ostrich egg is about 16 centimetres long and weighs as much as 1.5 kilos. That's more than 20 chicken eggs.

THE FACTS

The mammal that has the most babies at one time is the **common tenrec**, a shrew-like creature that lives in Madagascar. The tenrec has been known to give birth to as many as 31 babies at a time, but an average litter is about 20. The female has 29 teats!

The **cuckoo** is a bird with very unusual breeding habits. When the female is ready to lay eggs, she keeps an eye out for a suitable nest – a nest of eggs belonging to another kind of bird. When the owner leaves the nest to find food, the cuckoo swiftly pushes out an egg and lays one of her own.

A female **Nile crocodile** is a fearsome predator but she's also a good mum. Once she has laid her eggs – usually about 60 – she covers them with sand and stays nearby to guard them while they incubate. When the young are ready to hatch they start squeaking and the mother croc uncovers the eggs. As the babies hatch their mother picks them up in her mouth and gently carries them to water.

Amazingly, the cuckoo lays her eggs faster than other birds. Her egg even looks very like the others so the owner of the nest generally doesn't notice. The cuckoo egg is then incubated with the rest of the eggs.

The cuckoo egg hatches sooner than the other eggs and the young cuckoo may even push the other eggs – or the other young when they hatch – out of the nest. The cuckoo generally grows larger than its foster parent, which has to work hard to keep the intruder fed.

The world's biggest baby is the **blue whale** which measures an astonishing 8 metres at birth and weighs about 2.7 tonnes. For the first seven or eight months a baby blue whale feeds only on its mother's milk and drinks about 375 litres every day – that's three or four bathfuls. It gains weight at the rate of about 4 kilos an hour.

Most fish lay eggs, which drift and hatch in the water, but some produce live young. The **blue shark**'s eggs develop and hatch inside the mother's body and she gives birth to 25–50 young. Each baby shark is about 50 centimetres long.

Darwin's frog lives in deep forest in South America. When it's time to breed, the female frog lays her eggs on the ground, among dead leaves, and the male guards them. When the eggs are almost ready to hatch, the male picks up them up and takes them into a special throat pouch. There they hatch into tadpoles and remain while they grow into tiny froglets. The male lets them go when they are about a centimetre long.

Other sharks, such as the horn shark, lay eggs in tough egg cases to protect them while they develop. Each case contains one egg, which the mother wedges into a crack in a rock in shallow water to keep it safe. Spiral ridges on the egg case make it very hard for any predator to get at. The case contains a yolk sac, which the baby feeds off as it develops. It hatches 6–10 months later.

The **giant pacific octopus** is a very devoted parent. After mating, she settles in a cave in deep water and lays as many as 70,000 eggs. These hang from the roof of the den in long strands. For seven months the mother octopus stays with her eggs, fanning water over them and keeping them safe. She doesn't eat during this time and she dies soon after her eggs hatch.

Badgers live in family groups in underground homes called setts. There are usually a number of separate chambers or 'rooms' linked by passages, and several different entrances. Sleeping areas are lined with dry grass and leaves, and badgers may drag this bedding material outside in the morning to air.

Badgers like to keep their home clean and they have separate toilet areas near the burrow.

Have you ever wondered if a **hedgehog** is born spiny? A newborn hedgehog does have lots of spines but they are soft and under the skin so they don't hurt the mother. A few hours after the birth the spines come through the skin. The first spines are white, but brown spines start appear when the baby hedgehog, or hoglet, is a day or so old.

The **malleefowl** is a ground-living Australian bird and has a very special way of keeping its eggs warm. The male and female pair builds a mound of leaves and twigs. As the leaves start to rot, the birds cover them with sand to keep in the warmth.

The female lays her eggs in the mound and the male watches over them. He regularly checks the temperature with his beak and if the nest gets too cool he adds some more sand. If it gets too hot he takes some away. Amazingly he keeps the mound to 33–34 degrees centigrade while the eggs incubate for 60 days.

STEVE BACKSHALL'S
ANIMAL FAMILIES
WORDSEARCH

The names of 12 of the animals mentioned in this chapter are hidden in this wordsearch puzzle. Can you find them all?

n	o	c	t	o	p	u	s	t	z	j	r	c	l	l
t	i	b	t	x	q	i	x	b	v	d	e	u	s	c
k	w	l	h	e	s	c	a	a	a	s	d	c	b	m
v	r	m	e	c	n	d	o	r	m	c	k	k	z	y
h	f	a	e	c	g	r	w	u	h	r	a	o	l	p
q	f	w	h	e	r	i	e	c	l	d	n	o	g	y
e	d	h	r	s	n	o	i	c	y	z	g	o	o	u
f	e	m	s	s	e	r	c	p	v	g	a	i	h	h
f	s	i	f	k	t	u	y	o	n	c	r	r	e	g
n	o	r	o	s	n	j	l	u	d	s	o	p	g	q
l	o	k	o	w	a	x	k	b	v	i	o	p	d	d
g	c	e	u	i	r	y	a	i	z	r	l	f	e	s
a	a	b	t	g	k	v	b	x	c	e	v	e	h	j
e	l	a	h	w	e	u	l	b	n	m	f	i	r	i
b	e	e	h	u	m	m	i	n	g	b	i	r	d	z

**Blue whale, Red kangaroo, Tenrec, Ostrich, Bee hummingbird, Nile crocodile
Cuckoo, Blue shark, Darwin's frog, Badger, Hedgehog, Octopus**

RED KANGAROO

The red kangaroo lives in Australia and is the largest of all the marsupials. A marsupial is a kind of mammal that gives birth to very tiny undeveloped young. The baby then finishes its development in a pouch on the mother's body. There are about 250 kinds of marsupials. Most live in Australia and New Guinea, but there are also about 70 species in South and Central America and one – the Virginia opossum – lives in North America.

have large, powerful back legs and can leap along at high speeds. They feed on grasses and other plants.

The female gives birth to a tiny, blind, hairless baby that weighs under a gram – less than a grape. This minute creature makes its way to the mother's pouch all by itself – a journey that takes about three minutes. Once in the pouch, the baby latches on to a teat and starts to feed. There it remains for several months, feeding on its mother's milk and growing bigger.

The male red kangaroo is much larger than the female and is an awesome 2 metres tall. Both male and female kangaroos

Later, the young kangaroo, known as a joey, starts to poke its head out of the pouch and leave it for short periods – but at any sign of danger it swiftly hops back. By about 240 days the joey is ready to leave the pouch for good. It may continue to suckle for a while, though, even if there is another tiny baby in the pouch.

A male red kangaroo
can grow to 90 kilograms.

A kangaroo can bound
9 metres with one jump.

Kangaroos feed on
grass and other plants.

Kangaroos can give
powerful kicks with
their back legs.

Grey wolves hunt in packs and, working together, can bring down prey ten times their own size such as moose and caribou. Find out more about these amazing animals in my book *Wilds of the Wolf*.

The **harpy eagle** has 13 cm-long talons for killing its prey.

CHAPTER 4

FINDING FOOD

The magnificent **frigatebird** can catch its own prey, but it also steals food. It attacks other birds in the air, making them drop their catch, which the frigatebird then snatches.

Brown bears are expert at catching salmon as they migrate upriver. A bear may catch and eat as many as 40 salmon a day.

Army ants hunt in huge troops of 200,000 or more individuals.

THE FACTS

Some animals are very choosy about what they eat. The **koala** feeds mostly on the leaves of eucalyptus trees but only those of certain kinds. It eats about 500 grams of leaves a day and has specially shaped teeth to grind its tough food down to a paste.

The leaves are not very nutritious so the koala spends much of the day sleeping in order to save energy.

The **snail kite** is another picky eater. This bird of prey feeds on a particular sort of freshwater snail and its beak is perfectly shaped for removing snails from their shells. When hunting for its food, the kite flies above the water surface. When it spots a snail it grabs it with its foot, then takes it to a perch to eat.

The **giant anteater** is a big animal – up to 2 metres long and weighing up to 55 kilos – but it feeds mostly on tiny ants and termites. It may eat as many as 30,000 of these little insects a day. Once the anteater finds an ant or termite nest it tears into it with its strong front claws.

The **red fox** will eat almost anything. It is a speedy and expert hunter, catching rats, birds and insects, but it also steals from dustbins and compost heaps. City foxes will eat the remains of fast food dumped on the street. If a fox has more food than it can eat it will bury it for another time.

One of the fox's many hunting techniques is the 'mouse jump'. Having spotted a small prey, the fox gets as close to it as possible. Then it leaps up on its hind legs and jumps, landing with its front paws right on the victim – which has no chance of escape!

Lions are the only cats that live and hunt together. They live in family groups called prides, which may contain several females and their young, led by a dominant male.

The males may look big and fierce with their huge manes of hair, but it is the female lions that do most of the hunting. They work together, stealthily creeping close to their prey, then catching it in a final high-speed dash and pounce.

A lion may give a fearsome roar after a kill. This is a way of telling lions in other prides to stay away but the sound can also be heard by people up to 9 kilometres away.

Vultures are scavengers, which means that they feed on the remains of animals that have died naturally or on the leftovers from other hunters' kills. The **white-backed vulture** soars high over the plains of East Africa, searching for possible meals. When it spots something, it plummets to the ground but it also keeps an eye on other vultures. If one vulture sees another swooping down it suspects there is food to be had and swiftly follows.

Like all vultures, the white-backed has a powerful hooked beak that it uses to tear into carcasses. Its head and neck are almost bare of feathers. This is important, as the bird has to plunge its head into rotting carcasses. Feathers would be hard to clean after such a messy meal.

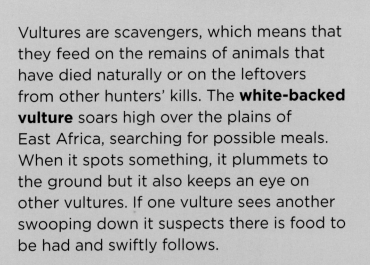

The **ogre-faced spider** makes a very special web for catching its prey. It spins a little net that it holds between its front legs. With the trap at the ready the spider hangs from a plant watching for prey. When something wanders by, the spider quickly hurls the net over the prey and wraps it up so it can't escape. The spider then bites its prey to paralyse it and enjoys its meal at its leisure.

The **western diamond-backed rattlesnake** kills prey such as mice and birds with its deadly venom. But as well as quickly killing its victims, the snake's venom also helps the snake digest its meal.

The rattlesnake has good senses of sight and smell but it also hunts at night using a very special sense. On its head are heat-sensitive pits that allow the snake to 'see' the heat given off by warm-blooded prey and track it, even in complete darkness.

A few animals use tools to help them get the food they want. **Long-tailed macaques**, a kind of monkey, have been seen using stones to knock oysters and other shellfish off rocks and to open the hard shells to get at the soft flesh inside.

STEVE BACKSHALL'S
FINDING FOOD
WORDSEARCH

The names of 12 of the animals mentioned in this chapter are hidden in this wordsearch puzzle. Can you find them all?

t	p	q	t	v	p	p	d	f	w	y	m	r	d	k
i	f	i	b	o	c	v	l	i	k	m	e	f	y	u
g	f	z	g	m	l	o	k	e	o	t	i	i	v	h
e	x	r	m	x	w	i	e	t	a	g	u	j	a	n
r	b	r	i	y	g	n	h	e	l	f	d	r	n	p
s	u	b	e	g	j	t	t	n	a	n	p	c	f	r
h	g	r	d	w	a	n	f	b	d	y	x	o	s	a
a	g	f	l	r	a	t	t	l	e	s	n	a	k	e
r	u	i	s	t	b	c	e	a	n	n	v	k	t	b
k	o	i	n	d	t	k	g	b	r	s	f	b	c	n
n	e	a	p	o	t	l	b	m	i	e	p	u	p	w
d	i	c	c	j	e	x	y	q	y	r	d	c	t	o
g	e	t	i	k	l	i	a	n	s	z	d	f	s	r
v	u	l	t	u	r	e	p	z	l	e	d	c	o	b
e	b	i	c	r	h	r	i	l	p	v	n	a	x	x

Koala, Snail kite, Giant anteater, Red fox, Lion, Vulture, Rattlesnake, Tiger shark Grey wolf, Harpy eagle, Frigatebird, Brown bear

STEVE'S SPOTLIGHT ON . . .
TIGER SHARK

This impressive predator is one of the biggest of all the sharks and has a fearsome reputation. It is second only to the great white shark for attacks on humans – but in fact it would probably much rather keep well our of our way!

The tiger shark has a big, broad head and a streamlined, tapering body. It preys on fish – including other sharks – as well as birds, dolphins and turtles but eats almost anything it comes across. Its teeth have super-sharp serrated edges, like a bread knife, allowing the shark to rip chunks of flesh from its catches. Its bite is so strong it can even crack open the tough shells of sea turtles.

Tiger sharks are also known to feed on dead animals and even swallow rubbish, such as sacks, cans and bottles. They have good eyesight and a superb sense of smell that enables them to detect the tiniest spot of blood in the water and trace the source.

Like all sharks, the tiger shark's body is covered with tiny teeth-like scales called denticles. These are very tough and so protect the shark from injury. They also help to streamline it and reduce drag as it swims, allowing it to move more swiftly through the water.

There's more about sharks and the dangers they face in my book *Shark Seas*.

Young tiger shark have stripy marking that fade as they grow older.

A tiger shark is about 4 metres long and 635 kilos in weight.

Tiger sharks live in tropical and sub-tropical waters worldwide.

CHAPTER 5

ANIMALS IN DANGER

About one in eight **bird** species are in danger of extinction and about one in four **mammals**.

A third to a half of **amphibian** species are in danger of extinction.

The world's rarest cat is the **Borneo bay cat**. Few have ever been seen and little is known about its habits

There are probably only about 3,200 **tigers** in the wild today – in fact, there are more tigers living in captivity than in the wild. Find out more about why tigers are so rare in my book *Tiger Wars*.

THE FACTS

Orang-utans are among the most endangered of all primates — the group of mammals that include monkeys, apes and humans. The two species live on the islands of Sumatra and Borneo in Indonesia.

There are about 54,000 Bornean orangs and the species is endangered. There are even fewer Sumatran orangs. Probably only about 6,600 remain so the species faces a high risk of becoming extinct in the wild.

Orang-utans live high in rainforest trees and feed mostly on fruit. The main reason they are now rare is the loss of their forest habitat. More than 80 per cent of the forests where they live has been cut down in the last 20 years.

Another problem is the capture of young animals for sale as pets, although this is now strictly against the law.

There's more about orang-utans and their world in my book *Ghosts of the Forest*

There are seven kinds of sea turtles and at least six of them are in serious danger of extinction. Marine turtles spend nearly all of their lives in the sea, but females come ashore to lay their eggs.

There are now only about 1,800 **giant pandas** in the world and three-quarters of these live in special reserves.

These big black and white bears live in mountain areas of south-central China in bamboo forests. Bamboo is their main food and they spend as much 14 hours a day munching away in order to get enough nourishment.

In the past, lots of pandas were captured by poachers but they are now protected by law. The other main problem has been the destruction of their forest home.

Once millions of bison roamed the prairies of North America. But so many were killed by hunters that by the end of the 19th century, it was 750. And the rest were built in the wild. Thanks to conservation efforts, there are now about 500,000 bison. But many of these are kept on ranches. More needs to be done to protect and encourage the spread of wild bison.

There are two kinds of rhino in Africa: the white rhinoceros and the **black rhinoceros**. Black rhinos are now critically endangered and only about 5,000 remain. Thousands have been killed by poachers for their horns, which are used in traditional medicine in Asia. Rhinos are now strictly protected but some are still lost to poachers.

The Kakapo is a kind of parrot but quite unlike any others in its group. It cannot fly and it is active at night, with it feeds on leaves, flowers, fruit and seeds. The birds used to live in New Zealand forests but they are now extinct on the mainland and are found only on a few offshore islands. Kakapos have suffered from the clearing of many forest areas. Large numbers were also killed by predators brought into New Zealand and by human hunters. Now only about 125 birds remain and all are carefully protected.

The **Ethiopian wolf** is the rarest of all the dog family. About 500 of these beautiful animals live in the mountains of Ethiopia where they hunt small rodents.

One of the main problems for the wolves has been that many have caught rabies from domestic dogs in the area. Conservation programmes have helped by vaccinating both wolves and dogs against the disease.

Lions once roamed all over the Middle East and India as well as in Africa. Now, **Asiatic lions** live only in the Gir Forest area in India and there are currently believed to be about 300 individuals.

Everyone knows that **African elephants** are the biggest of all land animals. Sadly the number of these majestic creatures are declining every day and probably only about 470,000 remain in the wild.

Even sharks could be in trouble. As many as 100 million sharks are killed every year, often just for their fins which are used in shark fin soup. Others are caught in nets and on lines set for catching other types of fish.

The scalloped and the **great hammerhead** sharks are both endangered, while others, such as the oceanic whitetip and the porbeagle, are vulnerable – their numbers are going down.

48

STEVE BACKSHALL'S
ANIMALS IN DANGER
WORDSEARCH

The names of 12 of the animals mentioned in this chapter are hidden in this wordsearch puzzle. Can you find them all?

u	n	o	e	r	t	e	m	k	s	r	k	k	z	a
v	y	o	e	l	q	m	a	f	n	t	r	t	a	d
f	t	g	i	o	e	k	d	b	e	s	a	y	d	l
b	i	j	a	l	a	p	p	q	o	u	h	q	n	h
t	e	x	o	p	c	y	h	r	t	p	s	y	a	e
g	p	d	o	o	e	i	e	a	w	q	k	z	p	d
e	l	t	r	u	t	c	t	r	n	q	i	k	t	g
a	x	u	j	g	o	h	n	a	v	t	d	n	n	e
f	l	o	w	n	a	i	p	o	i	h	t	e	a	h
z	f	t	i	h	v	t	n	o	s	s	v	p	i	o
w	c	h	h	j	l	e	e	t	t	i	a	b	g	g
y	r	e	g	g	n	c	o	j	j	k	b	w	l	r
o	r	a	n	g	u	t	a	n	f	j	g	i	d	e
f	o	m	f	c	e	w	m	l	a	z	p	x	k	t
p	y	f	r	y	w	z	i	s	x	e	d	e	t	z

STEVE'S SPOTLIGHT ON . . .
HEDGEHOG

[...] Britain's best-loved animals, the [...] is becoming worryingly rare. [...] show that numbers of [...] in Britain have gone down by [...] over the last 10 years.

[...] live in hedgerows and [...] well as gardens. They eat [...] such as worms, slugs [...] also feed on birds' eggs. [...] night and can move [...] quickly as they scurry around [...] food. Hedgehogs are also [...] In winter, when it is hard to [...] food, hedgehogs hibernate to save energy. They curl up in a leafy [...] quiet spot under a hedge or a sh[...]

Changes in the environment have [...] hedgehogs badly. More chemi[...] and pesticides, some of which [...] hedgehogs, are used on far[...] gardens and there are few[...] the animals to hide in. Ma[...] killed in the roads and in [...]

Ways to make [...] hedgeho[...]

• Don't use chemi[...] and leave a wild [...] corner with long [...] and wild fl[...]

• Make a comp[...] heap [...] creatures hedge[...] like to eat live [...] around compost he[...]

• Provide ho[...] such as special 'hog house' [...] pile of log [...] he[...]

Weighs up 2 kilos.

Up to 30 centimetres long with at tail of 1-2 cm.

Rolls itself up into a ball if attacked or frightened.

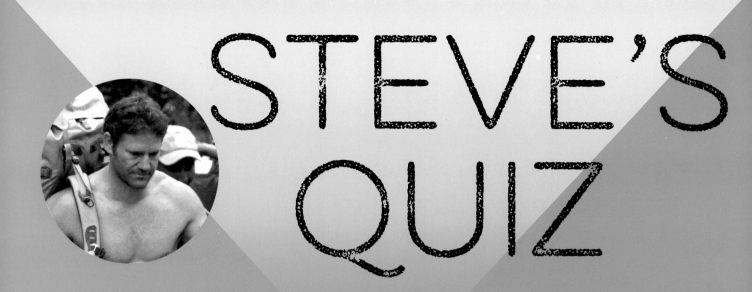

STEVE'S QUIZ

1 Which is the heaviest animal that has ever lived?
a African elephant
b Bronotosaurus
c Blue whale

2 How many tigers are left in the wild?
a 2,000
b 3,200
c 5,000

3 How tall is an emperor penguin?
a 1.2 metres
b 90 centimetres
c 2 metres

4 Which animal has the longest claws?
a Tiger
b Lion
c Giant armadillo

5 Where do gorillas live?
a Africa
b India
c South America

6 How fast can a hummingbird beat its wings?
a 100 times a second
b 30 times a second
c 90 times a second

54

7 Can flying frogs really fly?
a Yes
b No

8 How many legs does a house centipede have?
a 100 pairs
b 50 pairs
c 15 pairs

9 How long are a harpy eagle's talons?
a 13cm
b 5cm
c 20cm

11 How long is a tiger shark?
a 4 metres
b 6 metres
c 3 metres

10 What is a koala's favourite food?
a Ants
b Eucalyptus leaves
c Bamboo shoots

12 Which animals live in prides?
a Tigers
b Elephants
c Lions

13 Which is the largest sea turtle?
a Leatherback turtle
b Loggerhead turtle
c Green turtle

14 What is the kakapo?
a A kind of insect
b A kind of parrot
c A kind of snake

15 Which is the rarest member of the dog family?
a Arctic fox
b Fennec fox
c Ethiopian wolf

16 Which is the heaviest land animal?
a African elephant
b Black rhinoceros
c Giraffe

THE ANSWERS

BIGGEST, LONGEST, HEAVIEST
WORDSEARCH p17

ON THE MOVE WORDSEARCH p25

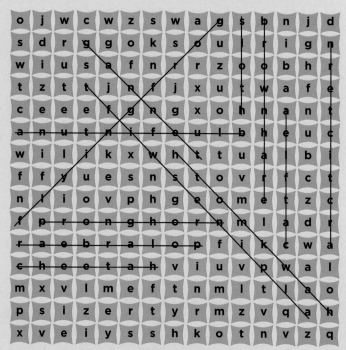

56

ANIMAL FAMILIES WORDSEARCH p33

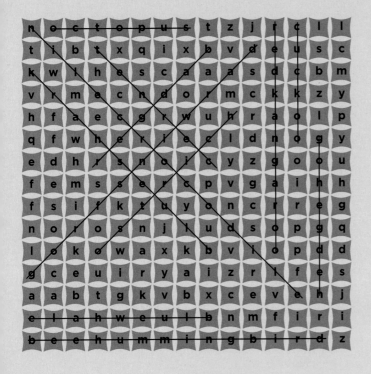

FINDING FOOD WORDSEARCH p41

ANIMALS IN DANGER WORDSEARCH p51

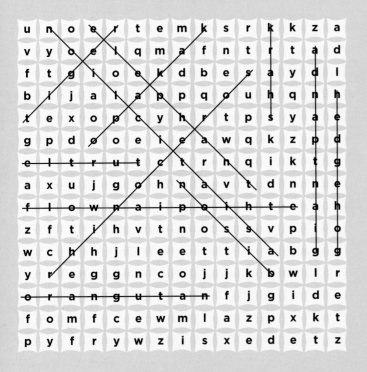

QUIZ ANSWERS

1 c
2 b
3 a
4 c
5 a
6 c
7 b
8 c
9 a
10 b
11 a
12 c
13 a
14 b
15 c
16 a

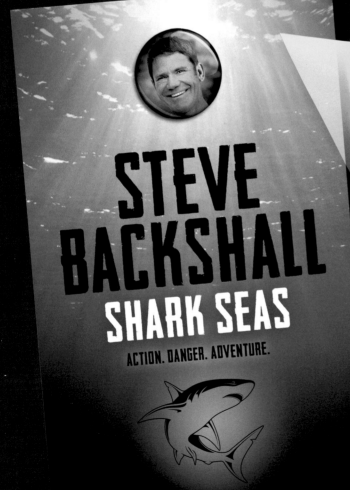

STEVE
BACKSHALL

SHARK SEAS

ACTION. DANGER. ADVENTURE.

FROM
OCTOBER
2016

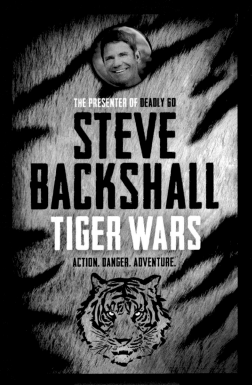

THE PRESENTER OF DEADLY 60
STEVE BACKSHALL
TIGER WARS
ACTION. DANGER. ADVENTURE.

OUT NOW

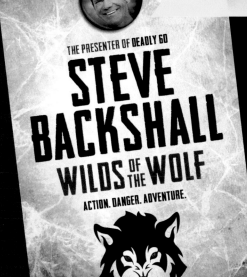

THE PRESENTER OF DEADLY 60
STEVE BACKSHALL
WILDS OF THE WOLF
ACTION. DANGER. ADVENTURE.

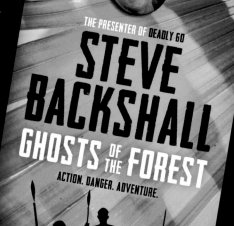

THE PRESENTER OF DEADLY 60
STEVE BACKSHALL
GHOSTS OF THE FOREST
ACTION. DANGER. ADVENTURE.

Join Steve Backshall as he comes face to face with the world's deadliest animals, in a book packed with fascinating facts, killer statistics and stunning photographs. Combined with his own incredible experiences with creatures, large and small, Steve reveals tricks of camouflage and feats of strength, endurance, teamwork and speed.

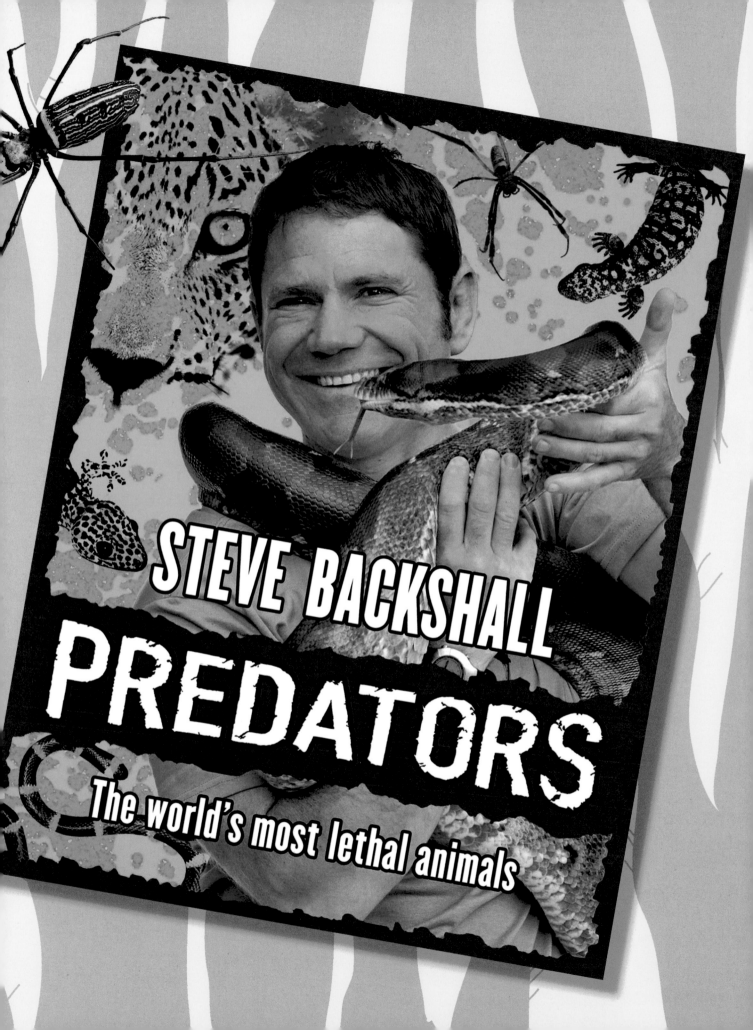

STEVE BACKSHALL

PREDATORS

The world's most lethal animals